Cowboys

By Philip B. Silcott
Photographs by Martin Rogers

■ BOOKS FOR YOUNG EXPLORERS
NATIONAL GEOGRAPHIC SOCIETY

A cowboy rides his favorite horse on a big ranch in Texas.
The cowboy's name is Mac Morrow.
His job is to take care of the ranch and all the horses and cattle.
Mac works very hard, and he stays outdoors most of the time.
Mac's horse works hard too. His name is King.
He can carry Mac for miles and miles on his strong back.
Horses need good food to make them strong.
They eat grass, and every day they also get a special meal of oats.
Mac scratches a horse on the head as he feeds him oats.

This cowboy has found a little lost calf and is taking it back to its mother. She is standing with other cows in the distance. A cowboy takes good care of the cows and calves and bulls.

4

He helps raise fat, healthy beef cattle to sell for food.
It is springtime on the ranch. That is when all the cowboys
ride out to round up the newborn calves.

Mac rides into a herd of cows, calves, and bulls.
He is throwing a rope to catch a calf.

It is time to take the new calves from their mothers for a little while.
The cowboys want to count the calves to see how many have been born.

Now the men have put
the calves into a pen.
The cowboys are waving
their arms and shouting
to make the calves go
into a cattle chute.
The chute is a narrow path
between two high fences.
The men count the calves
as they go through
the chute one by one.

At the end of the chute, each calf is caught and held tight
in a special holder. Then the calf is marked
so its owner will always know it is his. The mark is called a brand.
It is made with a red-hot tool called a branding iron.
Smoke rises as the branding iron burns some of the hair on the calf.
Did you ever see such a big needle for giving a shot?
The needle holds enough medicine for twenty-five calves.
As soon as the calves get their shots, they go back to their mothers.

A cowboy holds
a branding iron
before it is put
into a fire to heat.

A horse named Tiger kicks up a cloud of dust. He is inside a wooden fence called a corral. The man holding Tiger has a special job to do. His name is Alex Moses. He will put new shoes on Tiger. The new shoes will help keep Tiger from hurting his hoofs on the rocky ground.

With strong hands, Alex holds one of Tiger's hoofs.
He has already taken off the old shoe. Now he makes sure
the hoof is smooth and ready for a new shoe.
Horseshoes are made of iron,
and Alex uses a hammer and nails to put Tiger's shoes on.
Tiger stands quietly while Alex works.
The nails do not hurt at all. Finally all the shoes are on.
Alex uses a tool to file the hoof until it is smooth.
Soon Tiger will clop-clop away on his new shoes.

Sometimes horses get a ride too.
Mac and another cowboy are loading two horses into a truck.
Mac will drive the truck to a far place on the ranch
where there are cows and calves. There he will unload the horses
and put on their saddles for the day's work. Mac looks at
King's teeth to see if they fit together evenly. A horse must chew
well to keep healthy. Mac's wife, Karen, sometimes rides out to help
with the ranch work. Here she rides with her daughter, Katie.

Water for the cattle comes
from deep wells on the ranch.
A tall windmill pumps water
out of the ground.
When the wind blows hard,
it makes the big wheel whirl
round and round.
The whirling wheel
runs the motor
at the top of the tower.
And out of the well comes
cold clear water for the cattle.
Sometimes the windmill
stops working.
Then Mac climbs to the top
to work on the motor. Soon,
the wheel will be whirling again.

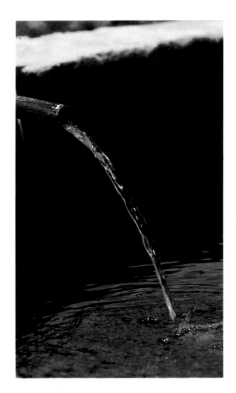

Brrr! In winter, cold winds sometimes
blow from the north. On a February day
Mac rides King out into a snowstorm.
Mac wears a warm jacket.
King has a thick coat of hair to keep him warm.
On cold winter mornings, water may freeze
in the stone troughs where the cattle drink.
Then Mac breaks the ice so the cattle can have
water when they are thirsty.
Katie and her two brothers,
Ben and Michael, help out.
Michael chips at the ice with a big stick.
Mac shovels the ice out onto the ground.

The ranch needs miles and miles of fences to keep the cattle
from wandering away. As soon as a fence breaks, it must be mended.
Mac finds a place where the fence has come loose from a post.
He ties it back with a short piece of wire. At another place
Mac finds a fence that needs to be tightened.
He fastens a tool to the fence and pulls on the long handle.
This stretches the fence until it is very tight.
When night comes, Mac builds a cheery fire and makes a pot of coffee.
After eating a snack, he will put out the fire and ride home.

With a short rope, Mac leads a young horse named Banner.
Someday Banner will be a fine saddle horse like King.
But first Banner must learn to wear a halter on her head.
Mac pulls her along gently so she will not be afraid.
Can you guess why Mac is putting a blanket on Banner?
No, it is not to keep her warm.
The blanket is there so Banner will get used to carrying it.
One day Mac will put a small blanket on her back,
and then he will put on a saddle like the one King carries.
But look out! The blanket is falling off!
Too late. The blanket has fallen to the ground.
Banner does not like the feel of it yet, and she hits at the blanket
with her hoofs. When she is older, Banner will carry her head high
as a proud cowboy rides her out to the roundup.

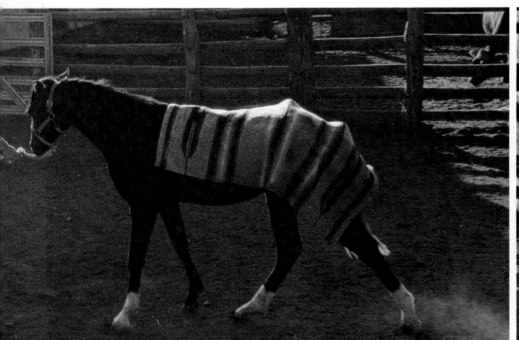

Mac rides fast through thorny brush, twirling his rope.
Why is he chasing the calf?
He can see that it has a disease called pinkeye.
To catch the calf, Mac throws the loop in his rope over the calf's head.
The calf is soon roped, and Mac and another cowboy
carefully put medicine on the eye. When they are finished,
the calf will jump up and scamper away.

Now Michael is going to try to throw a rope
just the way his dad did to catch the calf.
Michael makes a loop and goes after his dog Brandy.
Brandy just scoots out of the way.
So Michael goes after his dad—and catches him!
The rope tightens around dad's legs, and down he goes.
But it's all good fun, and Mac laughs as he hits the ground.

A boy chases a big calf.
He rides so fast
that you see just a blur.
Someday the boy may work on a ranch
of his own, and he must practice
riding and roping. He must learn
to mend fences, work on windmills,
and take care of cattle. Then one day
he will be ready to take his place
as a cowboy in the spring roundup.

Published by The National Geographic Society
Melvin M. Payne, *President;* Melville Bell Grosvenor, *Editor-in-Chief;* Gilbert M. Grosvenor, *Editor*

Prepared by
The Special Publications Division
Robert L. Breeden, *Editor*
Donald J. Crump, *Associate Editor*
Philip B. Silcott, *Senior Editor*
Cynthia Russ Ramsay, *Managing Editor*
Tee Loftin Snell, *Research*
Illustrations
Donald J. Crump, *Picture Editor*
Design and Art Direction
Joseph A. Taney, *Staff Art Director*
Josephine B. Bolt, *Associate Art Director*
Ursula Perrin, *Assistant Art Director*
Production and Printing
Robert W. Messer, *Production Manager*
George V. White, *Assistant Production Manager*
Raja D. Murshed, June L. Graham, *Production Assistants*
John R. Metcalfe, *Engraving and Printing*
Mary G. Burns, Jane H. Buxton, Stephanie S. Cooke, Suzanne J. Jacobson,
Marilyn L. Wilbur, *Staff Assistants*
Consultants
Mac and Karen Morrow, *Story Consultants*
Edith K. Chasnov, *Reading Consultant*

Little Ben reaches up
to give King a pat.
Ben can already ride,
but he cannot reach
high enough to get on
a horse by himself.
Someday he will grow up
to be a cowboy.
Then he will sit tall
in the saddle like his dad.